"PAST/PRESENT"   AND OTHER POEMS

Robert Kaplan
"PAST/PRESENT" AND OTHER POEMS

Poets of Queens Press
New York, 2023

Designed and composed by Oleksandr Fraze-Frazenko.

© All rights reserved. Printed in The USA. No part of this work may be reproduced or used in any form by any means — graphic, electronic or mechanical, including photocopying, recording, taping or usage in information storage and retrieval systems — without prior written permission of the authors, except for brief extracts for the purpose of review of this book.

ISBN 978-1-7351478-9-5

*To my parents, Harold Kaplan and Lore W. Kaplan.
Always.*

Acknowledgements

Several poems in this book have been previously published. My thanks to the editors, wherever they may now be:

"AIDS Death #54,911," *Beyond Definition: New Writing from Gay and Lesbian San Francisco.* Rpt. *A Loving Testimony: Losing Loved Ones to AIDS.*

"Avenue E," *Evergreen Chronicles.* Rpt. *KGB Bar Literary Magazine.*

"Diane," "Full Moon, July 1983," and "Rooster Poem," *modern words*.

Author's Note

As this is my first book, I'm going to indulge slightly. These poems are literally from another time, and figuratively from another place. With the exception of "Past/Present," they were all written during and about the ten-year period of the mid-1980s through the mid-1990s: some were written in New York; some in Tucson, in the MFA program at the University of Arizona; and some in San Francisco. "Past/Present" is about that same period of time; I began it in Tucson, worked on it further in San Francisco, and have revised it extensively over this past year. It was a raucous and rambunctious era. It is almost mythological, for me partially because I was much younger and but partially also because so much of that world is gone. Rent was cheap. It was possible to work less than full-time and have time for other pursuits. So many people died unnecessarily. Reading these pieces now, politically, it seems that very little has changed, even while so much has.

I have had so many lives since, it is impossible to thank everyone by name here. So some of you will have to wait until my next book, but know how important you are to me. For the revising and shaping and feedback on many of these pieces, and for all the poetic exchanges we once shared, I want to thank Patti Blanco, Barbara Cully, Sandy Florence, Boyer Rickel, and Karl Soehnlein. I want to express my tremendous gratitude to the indefatigable Olena Jennings, the editor of Poets of Queens Press, who plucked me out of obscurity when I began writing poetry again after a 25-year hiatus, and to Michelle Whittaker, who was so encouraging when I first tentatively opened that molding file folder on my computer and who has never wavered. For their friendship and support over many years, I want to thank Gennah Copen, Will Fisher, Liz Horwitt, Paul Lind, Marah Loft, and Nia Lourekas. And because it's important and right, I want to also thank Bea Krauss and Mark Prezorski.

Above all, I want to thank my parents, Harold Kaplan and Lore W. Kaplan, for their eternal love, even when they didn't understand; for instilling in me their humanitarian values and their passion for words and learning; and for their constant companionship. While no longer on this physical plane, our connection continues, and it is with deep deep love that I dedicate this book to the two of you.

Table of Contents

Past/Present *(Tucson and Manhattan, circa 1991)* **12**

Rooster Poem **45**

Yellow Ribbons, Trees, Etc. *(Winter 1991 - Winter 1992)* **49**

Full Moon, July 1983 **55**

Part of My History **56**

On Testing Negative **58**

Diane **60**

Avenue E **63**

AIDS Death #54,911 **67**

Past/Present
(Tucson and Manhattan, circa 1991)

Back in New York.
Back in that swell of cars and streets.
Sprung from the land of baked rock, baked sky, and blond hair.

It's the end of the long fall,
nights wrapped under the circular light
books splayed to their pages,
the grind and ground of academic chaff
kiss from the wide swanky desert
and I'm back walking up Second Avenue
wrapped in my long coat and scarf,
bags swung over my shoulder
and checking out boys:
their black leather jackets
their short dykey haircuts
the fact that none of them,
not one, are wearing any pink or green.

My shoes click against pavement.
Cold air tickles my lungs.
Buses sway in and out from the curb
and everyone's breath sways in front of their faces.
Three men walk by laughing, cheeks glowing, gloved hands slapping.
An old Ukrainian woman walks out of a store
wrapping her head in light blue scarves.
Cars point at each other, honk, swerve.

In that far away land sidewalks are long and empty
but here people surge over concrete
stand in doorways
talk, shout.
Oranges shine in a window.
Sun shines on lampposts and trash cans.
My bags swing against me.
Newspapers blow against each other.
I step off the curb, step onto the next,
step around a woman handing out flyers.
A man reads the paper inside a coffee shop.

Two men pass me,
blue woolen hats pulled over their heads
the backs of their jackets gleaming in light:
one half turns back, smiles,
the sun catches the hoops in his earlobes
and I catch my breath in my mouth,
I step off the curb behind him
my legs tickling with the flow of blood
the hint of sex
the thrill of a different kind of return.

Always, it seems, my lives keep bumping into each other.
Last summer I wandered these streets
caught in the pull of another distant, wavering man.
Even with 3000 miles still I hooked on impossible glimpses,
rising and fading in checkered light
like those far far away nights when bodily presence
whispered a wistful answer to some long hoped-for possibility.
I remember walking up out of the subway,
buildings and sky rising around me
trucks and cars spewing grit into the air
and the rumble of trains shaking my feet.
The front of my shirt was lined with sweat.
My shirt stuck to my skin.
Swirls of people down the steps toward me
faces glowing, shoes rat-a-tat tatting,
arms and shoulders bumping against each other, against me;
and then suddenly, one in particular,
a man with long hair, tall,
for a moment I thought something geographically impossible
and my breath, it stuck to my shirt,
and his shoes, they scuffed the steps.
I could hear a truck arguing with a pothole.
I could see the freckles on his nose his cheeks,
his eyes, no, not brown,
his hair, no, not pulled that way,
shoulders, calves, the slope to his walk,
no, not that,
still, even though he kept on walking
still, I had to look back.

All summer I kept looking back.
New York was porous, its center elsewhere.
I was porous, my center elsewhere:
sipping wine or reading a book or standing on a curb
waiting for a car to pass or drinking beer in a bar
my head tilted
watching the door, pushing inward,
I tilt the bottle, neck in my mouth, beer in my throat.

When the plane pointed itself back into the clouds
I knew those streets were on the other side
but when I again saw the continent they were miles away.

When I once had thought that that great big hunk o' land would
    solve everything.
Oh, how I once had thought that its enveloping distance was
    precisely what I needed.
Oh, how I once longed for that great big sloppy geographic kiss.

My last long ago night living in NYC.
Square zero.
Boxes glow in the street-lit dark.
Andrew's windows silhouetted across the street.
The Con Ed plant stretching its stacks:
red lights, silent tips, dark squares. My silent goodbye.
New York curled up, solid, breathing its breath.
I on its edge, standing, breathing my breath.
When I turn from the windows New York breathes at my back.
When I lie down New York whispers its storied, looking back
    backward sigh:
cold steps, cold door, cold tang of paint of turpentine,
my windows for so long with that same and always silhouetted gaze.

I pull the sheet over me,
imagine yellow earth, stabs of prickly green.

Oh, how I once had descended those steps ever so deliberately.
Oh, how I once had stepped down and down
as if each step brought me closer to some magnificent exit,
familiar cold door at that bottomy bottom
familiar cold parting at that spiky top,

clang of noise and motion clang clanging on the far side of that
    dark, silhouetted frame:
buses sighing, cars squawking, car alarms squawking back and back,
the clack of each step echoing its clackety clack echo.
Above me the single bulb muttered its mutter.
Oh, how the chair legs scraped the floor ever so ungratefully.
Oh, how he pushed himself into its single severe seat,
the radio, some music I couldn't quite identify,
it was all just noise now, just noise at my back.
Two years of this all-encompassing up and down
and everything that swirled around in those endless tides.

How innocent and quaint the before times now seem:
at my desk, banging poems into the wee of the night.
How was I to know how that sound sounded,
windows open, warm air rushing in, fingers pounding the keys?
Whenever I looked the buildings across the street were looking
    right back at me,
stores grated, humming gently to themselves some barely
    discernable tune
that I could never quite catch,
windows above them blank and not knowing how to respond.
Then one night I saw movement,
some mysterious man doing something that the windows
in their sudden modesty wouldn't reveal.
Of course I was curious so of course I watched.
And poems, of course I continued to bang on them.
And then that night at the bar when I saw someone up close and
    I had to find out.
He asked if I was the typist. I laughed,
and when I went to bed many hours later I knew that something
    momentous had just occurred.
Two years.
He brought me into his painting. I brought him into my words.
There was talk, laughter,
long nights in which too many cigarettes were smoked and much
    scotch consumed.
It was like receiving the best gift possible
whirls of color that provided purpose to every moment,
they changed how I moved in the world,

I who for so long had followed unguided and untethered
    wherever my instincts had led me
and now the wing opening, all my senses, my very breath.
How could I not fall? How could not he?
Even when I told him still he stayed, still close by,
almost but not quite.
*Because I finally realized that the inability to decide is its own
    decision.*

When I opened the door the big shiny street was stretched out
    around me in noisy exuberance:
people yelling, cars rattling, delivery trucks growling at each
    other, vying for attention,
back doors banging open, grumbling and snarling, then banging
    back shut.
It reminded me so much of how we would go at it:
the itchy build-up, the froth of release, sad lengthy apologies,
    rinse and repeat.
But now, now I was standing on the edge of a great big wide
    world full of lives going on
that had nothing to do with the one I call my own.
I couldn't help but smile,
wavy silky comfort stroking my cheeks.
Because I finally realized that bodily presence is only that.

I took a big breath, closed the door behind me with a deliberate click.
All that wavering, that relentless push and pull,
thrum of desire that wants to be reflected,
that is reflected, but not wide open and back,
at least not yet, at least not now.
Again and again, it rises and then the aftermath.
It was like an emotional tic
the air vibrating with what I too often had thought was simply
    finite indecision.
This time, I truly had thought it would be different.
Oh, for so long I had thought I could convince him of something
    spectacular.
Because I finally realized that I needed to stop.

I turned to my left to walk the quarter block home.
I wasn't still smiling, okay I was, a little, but I just felt
significantly and quietly lighter.
A big yellow taxi yelled out *Hallelujah!*
Another sped by screaming *It's about time!*
Of course I returned the gesture.
A green bus honked in celebration.
Rain dropped itself in long overdue delirium.
Unhooked, New York looked like it was floating on water.
Unhooked, I rearranged the furniture.
It's that tickling when something's due but hasn't quite yet arrived:
cars nuzzling up to me to drip on my shoes
streetlights waving me across soppy streets
bus stops glistening because they had something important to say.

Once light shortened then grew long then shortened then again
    lengthened.
Once the earth rotated, a couple of times, completed its cycle,
    again and then again.
The sun knocked on my window, handed me a message.
Unfolded, it looked like a cactus: purple, delicate.
Even though I had been waiting still I was startled.
It wasn't what I had been expecting.
I didn't know what I had been expecting
but this, I knew, wasn't it.

I stared at the sun; it stared back at me.
Are you sure, I said; *it's time*, it said.
I sighed, checked all the appropriate boxes, handed it back.
New York uncoiled, poked its head up to kiss me good-bye.
Yeah yeah yeah good-bye to you too.
My body kept running ahead of me
but I had to pack everything first
I had to rent a truck
I had things to say, people to say them to.
Streetlights kept waving at me.
Whenever I saw one I would smile demurely and just keep walking.

Oh, for the sweet caress of that moment when I thought that everything finally had shifted.
Oh, for that sweet sweet exhale when the sun wiggled its angle to wink ever so jauntily.
Oh, for that sweet sweet certainty that something shiny and kind had just been initiated.
Oh, for that surety propelling me so far far away to a place so full of possible newness.

Once light shortened then grew long then shortened then again
    lengthened.
Once the earth rotated, a couple of times, completed its cycle,
    again and then again.
Three summers passing. Three summers repeating themselves
    in spectacular grimy detail.
The plane pointing its right wing back into the sky.
The plane banking itself into and out from those old familiar clouds
stretching itself back out into its usual horizontal position.
Already those New York summer streets were ungluing behind me
yet still they kept troubling deep into my mind.
I kept seeing myself walking in what I thought was forward motion
and then an impossible flicker, and then something wavers,
something cracks, something echoes deep into the air.
I unbuckled my seatbelt.
The stewardess brought me a cocktail.
The sky held its final twinges
and I kept thinking about all those moments,
years of them really, lined up demurely like one long coy witness:
and then that deliberate click
and then those glowing boxes
and then again, so many times again after what I had thought
was finally square zero.
Another summer. Another ineffable and slightly porous summer.
And I leaned back into the cocoon of the airplane
watching the world slowly go dark, and I wondered what,
all these years, all this back and forth,
I had actually accomplished.

The moon swung out next to me.
Sometimes, down below,
lights would appear then disappear
and the engines would whir and subside.
I saw myself caught in that darkness and light
and I finally understood how much, how seductively, geography lies.
The plane would land, sleek and full of ineffable promise
and that faraway place would still be that faraway place:
dry earth, dry rock, hard little plants, and cacti rising up from the scrub
like wavy green people full of dry prickles and dry spine.
The rhythm of sun and sun, wind, and more sun.
How long it had been since the sun had knocked on my New York window.

How happy I was when I heard that rat-a-tat-tat on the crinkling glass.
I had almost started dancing, I was so impatient for whatever came next.
Even though its message puzzled me no end
still, I had known for some time that I needed to do something dramatic
and even if I didn't understand the particulars
I knew that it would never ever steer me wrong.

Little did I realize just how much more it knew than it was at the time letting on.

When I first arrived everything was so foreign:
scratchy earth, pastel clothes,
air vibrating with heat
wide white sidewalks that seemed to be laid out only for display.
And the boys, well, let's just say that it had been a long time since I had seen 22
and never ever had I seen blond. At least not naturally.
Even the sun didn't acknowledge that we had met before.
Whenever it thought I wasn't paying attention
it would look back over its shoulder at me
but no matter how often I waved at it or yelled out *Hi!*
or rode round in circles on my bicycle to try to get its attention,
not once did it give the slightest indication in public
that we had previously made each other's acquaintance.
It was so frustrating.
I didn't know why it was behaving that way.
Everywhere it was an overly large stark yellow
without a moment's consideration of how that might be affecting people.
Everything was so frustrating.
It felt like a scrim breathed imperceptibly between me and the buildings,
me and the people, the land, the very air I now somehow moved through
but no matter my efforts still it stuck to me: warm, undulating, and quietly humming.
Out beyond this odd, scrambled city
a ring of mountains jutted their stony fingers into every line of sight,
stripped of all pretense, solid and palpable.
No matter where I turned I could feel them staring at me, vibrating and merciless.
Out there too were the breathing bones of the deep dry desert,
they were always present, they were underneath everything,

they demanded attention,
but even though I understood that they were part of the bargain
how to give it to them, like so much else, was an anxiety-
   producing mystery.

Only the sky at night sometimes comforting,
rippling with stars that gazed downward stolidly, counseling wisdom.
I could sense something suspended among them,
emanating from a different future, if only I were to be patient,
which was not my strong suit.
Still, I knew that I couldn't undo what I had already done:
apartment sublet, papers properly signed.
I really had no choice but to trust that it would reveal itself
at what it considered to be the appropriate time.
I could only hope that it wouldn't be too long.

Oh, for that moment when the sun would finally take pity and pull me aside slyly.
Oh, for the revelations that would burst over me and make all this disconnect totally worth it.
Oh, for the promise of newness that would finally manifest itself in rich living technicolor.
Oh, for the turning of time into something long-awaited and magnificent.

Patience is a lesson learned like a pebble.
It comes in small hard lessons.

It was early evening,
the spring following the late summer of my strange arrival
and the winter of my discombobulation.
The oven door was slowly grinning its way back open
and I couldn't help but suspect that it was getting far too much pleasure
out of the misery that it knew it would soon be inflicting on people.
The sun had dipped behind those stolid mountains
darkening now with their inevitable angles
and behind them the sky streaking with flowering purple and red.
I knew those impassive figures held something that I couldn't quite yet articulate.
Behind them also wide miles of desert with so many unkempt promises.
And the wind, the wind blowing slightly,
at that hour still capable of providing a smidgen of coolness.
Fresh off those mountain backs it rolled right up to my cheeks,
beckoned demurely,
and for a moment I felt the breath of alternative molecules buzzing around me,
neutrons, protons, electrons lighting themselves like desert fireflies that do not exist,
and for the first time since I had arrived, I knew there was a next.

It all seemed so simple, really:
I and my fantasy VW Bug now come to yellow life,
a Super Beetle in fact, inches wider inches longer,
the two of us weaving our way through and between those squat stony mountains,
zooming round curves,
climbing hills because we knew we could,
cacti to the left of us, waving us past,
cacti to the right of us, cheering us on,
out and out into the broad sweeping spiny desert,
that swelling undulating chock-a-block desert filled to the brim with such delicious intention,
baking and breaking itself wide open just like the ocean,
waves and waves of it really, ready to jump in.
Oh, if only I had grasped this radiance so so much sooner than sooner:

windows rolled all the way down, hottish breeze blowing
   through with a hysterical overbite,
Joni Mitchell opining on the tape deck about big yellow taxis and
   paradise and pavement
and even though she was really singing about loss and regret
still, somehow, the beat, the upbeat, the guitar, the voice, the
   essence of Joni,
still, somehow, for that moment it all seemed to be just the right
   amount of right.
Once I learned how to shift without stalling from first gear into second
anything seemed possible.
After all, wasn't that what the sun had handed me when it had
   knocked on my window,
when I had opened it and the rattling sounds of cars, trucks, and buses
bounced off the floor and walls all around me,
wasn't that what I had received when I had reached out my hand
   to take what it offered:
yellow heat chipping away,
arms outstretched, face pointing outward,
ground breathing and firm underfoot, quietly insistent,
supporting me, nourishing me, up up from my core.
I thought I could write myself into it.
I thought that this could be the new narrative,
the in and out, the back and forth, that old repeatedly almost
   rising action
now distant and fading,
recurring appearances swatted away with a nonchalant flick of the wrist,
all hail the new emerging form, baked and solid!

Oh, for that possible future jangling its dusty pebbles all around and in front of me.
Oh, how I crooned and craned for it to come close.
Oh, how I breathed ever so deeply, swelling my lungs and my limbs to reach out and touch.
Oh, for that beautiful endpoint I could finally see dancing its slow dance just up the bend.

Patience is a lesson learned like a pebble.
It comes in small hard lessons.
Sometimes there are still more.

When I went again to the airport, oh so many times later,
when I boarded yet one more flight to the east,
I couldn't believe that I still was so capable of doing myself in.
I truly had thought that I was now expert at recognizing the
　　essence of vacillation.
I had so much experience sensing air vibrate in ways both dry
　　and alluring.
Yes, when his arm encircled me, I certainly enjoyed the touch of
　　skin on skin.
And yes, when he leaned in toward me, I certainly enjoyed that too.
I was well aware that these things happen sometimes,
had initiated them myself on numerous occasions.
It wasn't like he had tripped on something and fell toward me,
but really, what was the difference?
Each time I held out my arms I tried to make it mean only that motion,
no matter how pleasant, no matter how much it resonated
　　through all our interactions.
And when he unhooked, I simply went about life.
There was plenty to keep me busy and by this point I had plenty
　　of practice.
I was almost content.
But it was the sequel that got me,
when he showed up full of contrite intention until he wasn't,
even though, yes, I knew that I knew better.
Yes, I tried to unstring myself and to an extent I was successful,
quicker than ever in fact,
and the entire flight I kept telling myself that wasn't nothing,
but even so, even from 3000 miles, still his aura ricocheted
whenever the angles around me were just the right amount of right.

Even New York would occasionally express sympathy for my
　　situation.
What's three years, it would honk unprompted at me.
*I know how time works, the energy required to transform into
　　something new.*
Clearly it was trying to help me gain some perspective
rather than walk around all the time feeling vaguely sorry for myself.

Sometimes it would even blow newspapers in my direction,
whether to reinforce its point or to try to get me to lighten up I
   wasn't quite sure,
but either way I would kick at them or put up my arms to fend them off
and I couldn't help but laugh at the absurdity of the situation.
Whenever that happened something momentarily would settle,
which I assumed was the goal,
but whatever it was I could never quite pinpoint.

Oh, if only I could shake myself thoroughly and it would simply fall off the top of me.
Oh, for it to land smack on the sidewalk of humid 14th Street.
Oh, to bend down and finally recognize what, all these years, had been driving me to distraction.
Oh, to poke my foot at it and then kick it majestically far far away.

Patience is a lesson learned like a pebble.
It comes in small hard lessons.
But sometimes they do get answered.

Because now, now leaning deeper into the enveloping cocoon of
    that returning plane,
that purring perambulating plane wending itself deliberately
    and resolutely
through the trailing light of a flight back into the west,
engines breathing in a rhythm parallel to my own
and the darkness that settles slowly, inside and out and all around.
Because now, now breathing my way out over and across that
    living continent,
that undulating and checkered continent which is sometimes
    visible and sometimes not,
the atmosphere above it and whatever lay below,
New York curled inward and far far behind me
and I staring out at some hard geography slowly taking form:
my seat, the frame around me, the long metallic arc
all propelling me into a future that I know I do not want,
grinning face waiting to welcome me back
its jiggly arms and its all too familiar laugh.
I see it staring at me through the filmy surface of that pint-sized window,
that break-resistant artificial barrier hurtling through space,
and me along with it,
out into the panorama of what all these years had been, until
    now, resolutely hidden,
outside and in me, ticking my bones:
that revelation, no matter how expansive, is by its very nature insufficient,
that understanding, no matter how much it brings relief, is by
    itself never enough,
that even when the two make a joint appearance,
arms linked at the elbow, humming familiar show tunes
and decked out resplendently in the colors of the rainbow,
even then, they signify nothing more than another occurrence of
    that simultaneous arrival
which, while necessary and delightful, is simply an extremely
    dramatic moment,
one that many of us have experienced, perhaps more than once,
even while we tell ourselves that this one, this time, it really is different.
Extra special different.

It feels good. When it unfolds it glitters with the promise of so much joy.
It feels like something momentous either is happening or is
    about to happen.
But now, now pressed into the slight discomfort of that slightly
    too small seat,
cushion a bit lumpy, legroom almost an oxymoron,
cocktail and the food it made more palatable
all gone deep deep into the tubes of my body,
I see that the true import of that grand entrance is not the entrance
but, rather, the possibilities that linger in the afterglow of its
    fluttering wake;
those seemingly dazzling colors embedded in the armament of each figure
merely wavelengths of light refracting the cones in my eyes,
the physiology of energy
the biology of the body:
sensation, the retina, the nerves.

Yes, when I had descended those NYC steps
each one took me joyfully by the arm and guided me gently to
    the one below,
which was waiting so tenderly for me to feel its embrace.
Yes, they each whispered sweet nothings
and then handed me off with the tinge of a smile to the next one down.
And yes, the street that I then had crossed had gladhanded me
    from one side to the other,
clapping my back and encouraging me with abundant giggles
to slow down and truly relish this moment.
And also yes, when I had collapsed into the comfort of my own couch
stiff drink on the coffee table next to me,
scotch, of course, straight up,
two cats purring on my stomach and I exhausted in so many ways
but feeling so proud of what,
with some significant assistance, I finally had done:
the street laying itself down behind me, step by resolute step,
as a definitive marker of asphalt and concrete
not for him
not for any man prior
but for me, myself:
I, the recipient of the gaze that could mean so many different
things and often did,
simultaneously in fact,

and even then only for a moment before it turned into
something new
so of course I kept guessing incorrectly.
And even if I couldn't in that moment had known
how many more times I would repeat that behavior
still, I now had a frame of reference,
even if sometimes it only made things more frustrating
still, it was visible now, in the thick distance of that enveloping sky,
and I, I settling further into the muted glow of that pointed plane,
perched at the edge of some inner recognition
that all I had to do was note that I simply was being gazed upon
and then quietly remove myself from its presence,
however many times necessary,
with a small smile even if I so chose.
Nothing more.
Because it was always going to be nothing more.

And now, now with the fasten seatbelt sign lighting its sudden
    shine directly above me,
I see how much more fits into the back of a rental truck
than just boxes and furniture,
the space behind that waits quietly to be observed
the illusion of materiality tantalizing in its own magnificence.
It was me who had moved, but it was still me.
It is me.
Still.

When I got off the plane lightning flashed over the mountains.
The sky was flooded with planets and stars.
As always, they revolved so brightly above me,
shining their welcome back shine down on me
as I walked toward the parking lot,
bags swung over my shoulder, bags bouncing against my back,
I flashing again and again on what,
in and outside of that plane, I finally had perceived.
As always, they beckoned me to be bigger than myself.
So many times I had tried to do that,
stepping out into the silent night hours
to gaze up at those quivering points arrayed across space,
silent black sky pulsing and shimmering with the timed
    afterglows of spotted light.

I would close the front door silently behind me,
the silent city now even more silent,
silent streets silent buildings silent glistening sky.
So many lights, individual and shining,
no matter how many strands it took for them to arrive at my
    capacity to see.
It was always like seeing anew,
that sparkling sheen draped across wide and widening space,
hanging above me, just out of reach.
Dark buildings, dark trees, dark mountains silhouetted out beyond.
It was the opposite of emptiness.
It was an energy so palpable that my skin tingled, breathing its trace.
Always something inside me would breathe back, then go quiet.
I could feel it shifting, settling,
not quite ready to emerge.
It and my body waiting, wanting.
Wasn't this why I had moved all this distance?
Expansive light tapping something larger than myself
and I almost recognizing it,
out there, what I was searching for.

But now, now bags swaying and bouncing against my moving back.
Now I silhouetted inside and against the squared frame of the parking lot.
I now walking through and among lines of elevated light
shoes scuffing concrete and the sound echoing itself out
out into that otherwise silent and careening night
undulating far far above me
above the cars, above the concrete, the asphalt,
above this particular moment of this particular planet
gliding through this particular spot in space,
tiny circles pointing me toward that widening sheen,
the frame of my body
some inner sense pulsing with perception
pressing inside my skin:
I staring out into what had always been waiting,
patient and breathing, all these dappled years.
It's always nothing more.

Everything gone dark.
Everything glowing.

Perhaps when the sun had first appeared it purposely showed me just enough to get me moving.
Perhaps it knew that I had to think that I had done everything necessary for that to occur.
Perhaps if it had told me otherwise I wouldn't have believed it or I would have been so discouraged that I would have slid onto the floor and cried and drank myself into a puddle of scotch and cats.

Perhaps it's so much wiser than I have ever given it credit for being.

When I reached my car,
even though it had been sitting for three weeks gathering specks of desert dust
still, it started like it was just yesterday that I had closed the trunk and kissed it good-bye.
It wasn't magic,
the engine cranking to life
or I shifting smoothly into reverse, then into first, then second.
It was its way of giving me a hearty welcome.
It kept asking what had taken me so long.
I couldn't stop smiling, gliding past stationary objects like they were mere playthings.
It all seemed so simple, really,
the parking lot smooth underneath without a single bump to get in my way.
It was hard not to wonder why I was always the last to know.

Each day after that,
all that fall,
through classes and papers,
I kept feeling it:
light, air, dry, wind on my skin, rock dirt sun, feet on the planet, legs up from the earth,
exhaling, earth under me, always something under me,
solitary, solid, pointed, *yes*.

When it was time again to go to the airport
my body marched unerringly through the security gates
placed itself in its window seat
and announced that this time things really were going to be different.
I myself wasn't so sure
but when the plane picked itself up
it leaned over on one wing
and reminded me that every time it had seen me
I had been lost in the pull of some wavering man
and this time no one was pulling me anywhere.
Keep your seatbelt fastened, it said,
it's going to be a different kind of ride.
What could I do but lean back
and try to envision some unknown future:
New York, apartment empty,

the gift of subletting to someone on a parallel calendar,
but still I felt something familiar settling in:
when I had closed the back of the rental truck
and driven onto the interstate feeling like New York was just one big dead end.
Down below the United States of America was stripped of anything translucent
but the plane kept whispering its reassurances.
When it flew over Manhattan
I felt the promise of those glamorous buildings
and I realized that maybe it knew something that I didn't.

The engines purred in my ears.
My seat vibrated beneath me.
I put my tray table into the upright position,
pressed the button and my seatback moved forward.
I closed my eyes for the landing.
By the time I reached Second Avenue
my arms were churning
and I didn't know where to look next.
I kept moving around people and cars.
I kept looking at men.
My body still knew how to do it.
The man with hoops in his ears smiled at me.
The men, the motions,
the shapes of buildings.
His hoops tiny circles.
My legs rising and falling.
Cold air in my lungs.
Everyone's breath in front of their faces.
A car honking at me to cross the street.
Everything: the cars, the buildings, his hoops, his smile.
My feet bumping against concrete, against asphalt.
People coming at me from odd directions. Everything.

It's when I reach the outer edge of my old block that I finally realize that I'm on overload
and I just have to stop,
so I put my bags down on the sidewalk in front of me,
and I breathe, I breathe it all in.

Yes, people have to walk around me but at that moment I don't care,
the air a dome of cold and the sun so yellow, glowing on everything.
Teenagers yelling and laughing on their way out of school,
twenty somethings smoking their cigarettes and pretending to
   be imperturbable,
random middle-aged men and women swaddled in layers
and weighted with bags from the supermarket still across the street.
The obligatory car honking.
A bus pulls to the curb, exhaling and inhaling well-wrapped
   bodies clutching their hats.
The traffic light still turning colors.
The corner still pointed and smooth.
From the far side I watch it, consistent and measured,
directing traffic, holding back pedestrians,
and only when the light changes or there's a gap between cars,
even momentarily, only then letting them go.
Suddenly my body shivers, but it's not from cold.
It's the realization of how much I have missed that quiet
   thrumming:
its fluid movements,
the way it multitasks
and never misses a beat.
When it nods at me imperceptibly it grins slyly
but never takes its focus off the task at hand.
I didn't even realize that it had seen me
or how long it had been observing
but nonetheless I can feel the opening,
its warm embrace underneath welcoming me back
and I can't help but smile, pick up my bags, cross the street, and go.

Wind rattles the pizza sign directly ahead of me.
I wonder if their slices are still cheesy
and I feel that familiar surge.
I start walking faster now,
destination far corner
shifting my bags, first one shoulder, then the other:
Chinese take-out, empty store, donuts, psychic reader.
Corner getting closer.
People coming at me from odd directions.
Feet bumping against concrete:

fried chicken, empty store, used junk, bar, bodega.
Corner almost there, red light spotting me, waving me closer,
    opening its arms,
and then there I am:
ensconced in the warmth of its familiar click
my bags my feet
my old building facing me.
My old building. Still here.

A car rattles up to the light.
Somewhere someone is playing a radio.
The noise of the city hangs in widening circles
but here, here in their bell-like center
I face some other self stepping out through a door flung
    suddenly open,
standing on the stoop
looking down the street
stepping down the two cracked steps:
my body a pointer,
and bricks, a stoop I have walked up and down so many
    countless times.
I face my old building
bags over my shoulder
bags swinging against my back
the stoop I have
the street I have the door
the plane depositing me at the terminal with one long metallic kiss
whispering its final words of welcome and encouragement
then propelling me out into that sweet motion of life as it
    promises it will once again finally be
until, mere hours later, with a smooth sweep of its wrist
life peels itself back the way someone whose back is already out the door
for one moment still seems to stand in the doorway looking in
    multiple directions,
and then the air reconfigures itself:
the doorway empty
vibrations underfoot as a truck rumbles to a stop.

I open the door.
The hallway stretches in front of me.
A few more flecks of paint.

A few more stains in the stairwell.
The echo of shoes against tile.
The stairs at the far end.
When I reach them I imagine someone barreling down
legs poised head forward
the look of surprise
Hey, you're back
hugs kisses coats bags arms
because we're friendly, you know, we're a friendly building:
when the heat goes out
when the hallways go dark
when the garbage piles up
we're very very friendly,
we get our rent reduced
we stick together
we know our rights;
but the stairs are empty
echoing, familiar, tactile, and empty,
and my feet echo against tile
and everything looks oddly stark:
dirty white walls, peeling white ceiling, brown metal doors,
    rusting iron banister
all well-worn, framed by whitewashing light
that seems even more skeletal than I remember.
I continue climbing. My left hand grips the banister.
My body still knows how to do it:
each step like some other step,
the landing, the stairs all odd and funny and just achingly familiar:
my old building,
and stairs and walls and paint and stickers on apartment doors
and cars honking out in the street
and the vague sounds of music
and a television blaring
and the echo of each step
and the window facing the airshaft
and the light on my landing buzzing
and the way I used to run up and down.

When I stand in front of my apartment
and the key clicks into the lock
it's like I'm going forward and backward at the same time.

Then I walk inside and
it's even more mixed up:
the hallway still long and gray
and the kitchen floor still tilts,
but Dan's repainted the walls
but my paint's underneath his
and the cracks are the same.

The living room flooded with light.
The archway dividing it from what I called the study.
Because then it sounds like four rooms.
The old bookcases, the desk battered and shining.
Because I wanted to travel light into my future.
The square of the bedroom
shelves on the walls
the floor shining its familiar patchy shine.
No cats yawning up at me.
A couch—a different couch—under the windows
and behind it the radiator banging ecstatically,
the lamp Andrew made me now dusty and black
the little black metal table dusty too but no paintings on the walls
no cigarettes no bottles of flat cheap beer.
I throw my bags onto the couch, throw my coat over them,
and then I don't know what to do.
A drink seems most sensible
but it's the stillness,
the way silence and noise
hang in the air with such aching familiarity:
outside a car loud and insistent
but in here it's only me moving,
the click of my shoes against the wooden floor
and when I stop I can feel the air quivering,
if I could pull it back this would be my apartment, my home,
but I've moved thousands of miles
but the desk where I banged words into the 3:00 a.m. New York
    glowing darkness
but the archway where I hung plants until the cats began to chew:
New York, my old home,
the way my fingers touch the wall and know just how the cracks
    got there
the way every block held some kind of promise

walking through night streets
shining, full of motion,
sexy, tantalizing, alive.

I walk under the archway and over to a window.
Outside the streetlight is red, a taxi waiting.
Andrew's windows look at me.
For a moment I think I see him,
moving around, but then I realize it's just light on the glass.
A different liquor sign across the street
and it's more than three years now anyway.
More than three years.
Because one night I walked down those stairs
and I closed the door with a penultimate click.
The slamming of metal doors,
shouts and the wheezing of a bus sidling to a stop.
Because one night a bus honked in celebration.
Because once I thought it was him.

Last summer when I got off the plane
for the first time I noticed that the mountains were upright as buddhas
but on the drive home they kept telling me this riddle
about the importance of memory.
And the plane, just hours ago,
it kept on insisting that I should expect the unexpected
but it wasn't until my body started keaning at all that architecture
that I realized it was some past possible New York suddenly so
   very present.

I put on some music, lie on the floor,
stare at the dog on my ceiling,
the paint chipped just the right way.
Cold air rattles the windows.
The radiators bang out heat.
When I think of Arizona
everything feels far away and simultaneous
and I'm not sure how to react.
I run my hand along the molding,
press the back of my head against the floor.
I see myself wandering that strange heated earth
stark in my dark colors and dark hair.

I see the clarity that comes from that lack of distraction
but there's something else I see now too:
those nights I would lie here,
drinking or smoking and staring at the ceiling;
sitting at my desk
and the traffic light clicking red yellow and green
everything long and silent
only my fingers banging into the dark of the air;
walking down Second Avenue on a Friday night
and the sweep of lights and streets promising everything;
bumping into Brian
and slipping into a doorway
then slipping back here to roll on the floor;
Steven and I stumbling into a bodega for cigarettes
John and I stumbling into a bar for a beer
Steven and I sitting on his fire-escape talking about love
John and I lying in bed
toes fingertips tongues touching wherever they could;
tripping with Michael
and he said the moon looked like a 4
and I put my arms around him and wanted to never let go;
Alan and I on the dance floor, laughing,
leaning into each other, kissing and laughing,
then running, laughing, all the way home;
those boys, named and unnamed,
my hands on their backs
in their hair,
their eyes open their eyes closed
their heads rising between my legs
my head rising between theirs;
Andrew stepping in front of everything,
for such a long time he stood in front of everything
that only now am I remembering
there was a time before him that I forgot.

How much else have I forgotten?
Benny and Gino in the apartment next door,
2 alcoholic old men
who had no electricity
so they would leave their door open
and invite me in for a drink.

Their apartment smelled so much
that I'd sit in the hallway instead
and they'd tell me stories about the War.
Benny died on the front stoop
and Gino died in his bed
and for 2 days no one noticed
until Nancy and I knocked and knocked.
Mary and her dog Bunny,
Mary whose legs hurt so much
she'd climb the 5 flights one breath at a time.
One day I came into the building
and heard her puffing and cursing above me,
I caught up with her on the second floor
and carried her bags the rest of the way.
Bunny wheezed to the door to meet us.
Mary sat me down at the kitchen table and said,
"I know what you are. And I want you to know
you're like a son to me,"
and 3 weeks later she was dead,
at 75 she was dead and there was no one to claim anything.

All these memories
and I almost feel like I live here
but I don't.
When I walk into my old bar I know only the bartender,
good old Greg, who I've known since 1978
when we both lived in Boston, on the same street,
one block apart.
Greg, who gives me free beers which he no longer drinks
and with whom I talk, each time, about how everything is
    different:
his sobriety, his lover's death,
the apartment he moved out of;
my living in Arizona,
loving the desert missing the city
feeling out of place in both places
but I'm teaching I'm writing
I'm focusing my life.
Always there's good music on the jukebox.
Always I wish there was a place like this in Tucson.
Always after 3 or 4 beers I realize

that these urban boys are talking to each other
and I'm doing something else.
So I kiss Greg good-bye
and our tongues touch slightly
and I wonder if we'll ever have sex
and I lie in bed
looking at the cabinet that Tony said he'd build me
while Daniel and Steven sat on my couch
looking at proofs of our magazine
arguing about the cover
then going home to make up.

Now Daniel is dead and Steven is dead and Jackie
and Anne and Rick and Eddie and John and so many others
whose names I can't remember.
Some of them were queer, some of them were junkies,
some of them were both
and none of them deserved it
and I wonder, once more, why they are and I'm not.

I climb out of bed, sit at my desk to write some stuff down.
Each day seems to start isolated from the one before
but when I write I realize that's not true:
when I packed up that truck and drove into the spine of the continent
I thought only about what lay west of me
not realizing I'd be back in these rooms
still shaking off the consequences.
Tonight I thought I saw Steven on the street but I knew that was
    impossible.
Then I rounded a corner and there was Michael,
leaning against a building
eating a slice of pizza:
cheese was dribbling off the side
and he smiled and wiped his mouth
and we walked a few blocks together,
even exchanged phone numbers,
but I knew neither of us would call.
Just before sunset I walked down to Tompkins Square Park
and saw the fences put up
to keep out the homeless.
Inside were two bulldozers, yellow and motionless,

their blades silent
touching each other.
Bark was peeling off the trees
the sun was scraping at metal and dirt,
and I remembered Daniel and I
sitting on a bench
while Alice played with the other dogs
and the pigeons cooed in the bushes
and he cooed about Steven.
Tony and I were drunk early one morning,
walking down St. Mark's Place
with our newspapers and our coffees
discussing nothing,
the street wide
the sun shining
a couple of cars rattling and bouncing
and one old man snoring red-nosed on a stoop.
When we entered the park
to veer off in our opposite directions
we both stopped just as we rounded a bush
because there, at 5:30 in the morning,
in the midst of dog shit and bottles
were all these tulips,
these waving circles of red and yellow
and we knew then that there was magic still,
at this moment, in this place.

It's the way I would sit at my desk late at night
and the buildings would rise up long and silent
and the windows across the street were just windows
and the street was quiet and dark
and the yellow stripe shone like the moon grinning behind the
    Con Ed plant
and my fingers moved across the alphabet, banging out line after
    line.
It's the place I try to imagine,
not knowing the next word.

Rooster Poem

It's Wednesday afternoon and the improbable rooster is crowing.
Persistent, diamond-shaped, probably illegal,
it leans, I imagine, back on its haunches
behind the fence
across from my house,
points its beak at that round Arizona sun
and belts out its rooster sound
loud enough for every rooster on the planet to hear,
crowing itself into some heightened form
of rooster-altered consciousness
while I stand at my front door
jamming my key into the lock
and wishing that I could scream just as loud;
then I slam down the sidewalk kicking
at aluminum cans,
fling rocks into an empty lot,
pace in and out of stores,
call my phone machine from the pay phone a block away
and hold the phone to my face
while that sun burns the skin off of my hand
and I stare back as if to crow it down from the sky;
it's when those three sharp beeps
squawk from the other end
and I slam the phone back onto its silver hook
and kick the metal pole underneath,
it's then that I see myself rising into that elongated reflection,
arms extended
legs at different angles
my entire body puffing out,
and I realize how I must have looked
when I leaned over the stove
frying onions and you asked if it would be all right if we were friends.

I could hear everything popping and sizzling:
the wooden spoon beat against the pan,
the flame sucked on gas,
my bones swelled and cracked as I took a deep breath
and thought that for once I would try to just keep on moving;
I could hear your skin folding around you

I could hear my skin folding around me,
when we later walked outside
I was already watching the clouds getting more solid,
I was watching your promise of a phone call or anything else
ricochet back where it came from,
I could feel that familiar miserable yowling
start its slow climb
up toward my mouth
and when you waved good-bye
I was already humming that song
of one more man who done me wrong,
and even though I never actually sang it
when I see myself rising into the glory of that shining pay phone
which is gleaming in metallic splendor
I see precisely what,
whenever you looked at me,
you must have seen:
my mouth open
my throat engorged
my head swaying back and forth
just like that rooster
who is strutting and preening
and kicking up pebbles and dust
because he and I have the right to have anything we want
and you are breaking the rules by not cooperating;
and I settle back onto the ground
and look up at the sky
hoping to find something in all those blue and yellow lines
because no, I do not want to act like this,
and I'm not quite sure how to stop.

So I start walking the round walk of the ruminating,
round sun looming over me like one eye of the rooster,
shadow following behind me like some shapeshifting rooster
nipping when I least expect it;
don't want to admit
that you sliding away is not the greatest tragedy;
happens, in fact, quite regularly:
two people meet each other,
spend some time,
only one decides he wants something serious.

Don't want to admit that's pretty ordinary.
Who wants to be ordinary?
Not when I can carry on in that grand old homosexual style
for which we are so well known,
insisting that I deserve endless sympathy
perpetual flowers
the right to be bitchy as all hell
and the right to mourn you longer than I knew you;
not when I can *kvel* like an immigrant Jew
and be loud and make noise and chicken soup
and beat on my chest and feel guilty
because I should know better than to trust the *goyim*;
but walking under that widening rooster eye
I see myself walking out of my house:
the world smiles at my white feathers,
the cars whisper approval,
the sidewalks grant me a certain surety and grace
a certain *je ne sais quoi*
when I strut to the corner with that red-combed rooster strut
and the houses nod their windows
and the streets line up accordingly
and the signs all make sure
they're pointing in the proper direction
and still you won't give me what I rightfully deserve.

Now I feel that rooster eye shimmering toward me
and I can't help but wonder
what the difference is
between my yowling at the stove
and my strutting down the street:
when a woman says no
and the man thinks she means yes,
when those pioneer roosters swarmed westward over
the Atlantic
the Appalachians
the Mississippi
the Great Plains,
where precisely does difference lie?
I feel that rooster breath on the top of my head.
I feel those rooster feathers sliding into my hair.
I think of other roosters

goose-stepping across Europe,
my mother and her family sitting in the kitchen,
quietly,
and even with the windows shuttered
and her mother placing a large hand
around her small one,
pressing it, gently, against the table,
still she can hear the click of boots against pavement;
even when she and her family slip
westward
over the Atlantic,
still it happens again and again
when I hear of the man who walks out of a gay bar
and the bat and the black rooster boot come down.

Always I think about that:
the hush of a dark street,
the long piece of wood,
the shoes skimming concrete;
always I need to know exactly where I am.

Is it possible to lie down with my rooster,
to cradle him in my arms
and tell him that yes, I know exactly why
he is making such a ruckus
but there are times
when we simply cannot have our way;
to place my hand on top of my mother's mother's hand
so that my mother's hand is now enclosed
by ten fingers
and the windows shimmer around us
and I tell her that we are all afraid;
to kneel down next to that man
who is leaking all over the sidewalk,
wrap my arms around him
and whisper that he is brave?

Is it possible to look into that shimmering rooster eye
and not be afraid of what will look back out?

Yellow Ribbons, Trees, Etc.
(Winter 1991 - Winter 1992)

I.

Whenever I see yellow ribbons
I see yellow stars:
I see old Jews hunched at the waist
middle-aged Jews with skin pulled over their bones
young Jews whose lives are a pinpoint in their eyes.

Whenever I see yellow slips of material
snaking around trees and doorknobs
I see lines of Jews snaking across Europe:
I see disappearances, round-ups,
Jews of all ages snaking toward Auschwitz
toward Birkenau toward Bergen-Belsen
Dachau Dora Ravensbrück.

When I hear on the radio
that we have kicked the Vietnam syndrome
I think of my mother on a boat
because Germany would never again be humiliated,
I think of Weimar
of Panama
the Anschluss
Grenada,
I hear Saddam pronounced Sodom
and I think of Jews hoarding all the money
Jews the center of an international conspiracy
Jews a cancer on the moral fiber,
and I leave my house
making sure that my long nose is tucked safely in my pocket
my $1000 bills stuffed in a teapot
my horns left on the night table
because when I leave my house
stars and stripes sprawl across almost every windshield,
stores bend under signs that proclaim, "We Support Our Troops,"
yellow tongues swell and flap on trees and doorknobs
and everywhere everything mutters
that I am a Jew for my religion

a Jew for my pinkocommiequeer
a Jew for my opposition
a Jew for my memory,
and my Jewish shoes click against the sidewalk
and my Jewish teeth click against my mouth
pieces of yellow fabric click against themselves
yellow airplanes click against the open sky
yellow train doors click open and shut
the world opens its yellow wings
and the yellow wings unfold with the sound of bone clicking
against bone,
the yellow wings unfold with the sound of the silencing of the Jews.

II.

What does it mean to be a Jew?
To haggle and bicker and want ten pounds of flesh:
this is one piece.
To see the hood closing over the head
the head smiling
the mail opened
to hear the knock on the door:
this is another.

I am at the anti-war rally.
I see speakers
signs
people sitting on grass.
I am standing behind a woman with long brown hair
she is nodding her head
she is standing next to a man who looks somehow familiar.
I see the other crowd pushing forward
holding a flag
filled with white stars
and I think: this is one piece more.
I think: this could be Berlin.
I think: this could be Selma, Alabama,
or Wichita, Kansas,
or Williamsburg, in Brooklyn,
where right now Hasidic Jews are patrolling the neighborhood
to keep an eye on the darkies

and I remember reading that once Jews and blacks
made soup together,
I remember reading that in 1909 Jews helped form the NAACP,
that in the 1950s, in the South,
temples were bombed, Jews were murdered,
all this because Jews spoke for desegregation
all this because Jews helped register Negro voters,
and when I then read that in Israel
the government is keeping gas masks
from Palestinians
I start opening books trying to find
where all those other Jews have disappeared.

When I walk into my class
I ask my students how many were taught about the Montgomery
   bus boycott:
eight raise their hands
six say they aren't sure
one says that something about it sounds somehow familiar.
Then I ask when the Montgomery bus boycott was
and two say they think it was in the late 1960s
and one says it was earlier than that
and the rest have no idea.
None have heard of the Palmer Raids.
Two have heard of the Hollywood Ten.
Four know that Japanese-Americans were put into internment camps
and I stop asking questions
because I see just how complete that disappearance is.
Then I remember that when the Gulf War started
I asked how many were for it
and everyone raised their hand
except one teenager
who placed both of his on his desk
and looked at those arms,
all around him,
raised upward.
He and I looked at each other
from opposite sides of the room
surrounded by hands.
Now I understand the purpose that that disappearance serves.
But when I then hear that in the Bronx

just three weeks ago
two black children were surrounded by four white teenagers
who poured white paint over their heads their faces,
who said they did this so those children could have the experience
    of being white,
so they could walk into restaurants without people checking
their wallets their pocketbooks,
I want to grab onto my white skin
I want to slip into that soft yellow
fluttering on trees
and hair,
I want to hide that which can never really be hidden:
the nervous twitch in my fingers
the way I move my hands
my tongue that keeps jumping out from behind my teeth
and those incorrect words that constantly slip off of it.

Sometimes when I am nearing sleep or in the morning,
over coffee,
wrapped in the comfort of blankets and ritual
I try to imagine that easy glide
and I know that if I do not open my mouth
if I do not move my body in particular ways
that smooth arc can be mine.
I know also that there is a difference
between having to and wanting to and not being able to
but when that other crowd moves forward, shouting,
in unison,
one simple word
and that one word is louder
than any one man or one woman and one microphone,
which of those three stances is the one I can call my own?
Do I slip into that other crowd and hope to disappear?
Do I sit on the ground and cover my head?
Do I link arms with the woman in front of me
and she with the man next to her
and all of us, slowly,
turn to face those who would silence us
because, in that fine Jewish tradition,
we have read the fine print?
When, then, can I play out that other story,

the one where I ask each of my Jewish friends
why their families left Europe
and they do not all tell me the same thing,
the thing I already know from asking both sides of my own?
When do I get the opportunity to play that other story out?

III.

I am thinking about lies:
big lies, little lies,
lies that had roast beef,
lies that had none,
lies that land behind enemy territory
and make their way all the way home.
The Jew thinks about these things.

The Jew thinks about Nayireh crying before Congress
that Kuwaiti babies were thrown out of incubators by Iraqi brutes,
sees the long shadow of oil shining behind her ears
sees the men glistening in that serious distance:
Nayireh, 15-years-old,
she who burrows into sand and leaves no trace.
The Jew thinks about lies.

The Jew is intimately familiar with lies:
the Bubonic Plague
the Reichstag Fire
the Watts Riots
Stonewall Riots
the Intifada
the Chicano Moratorium Against the Vietnam War
ACT-UP and the Women's Health Action Mobilization! stopping
    the Church
Wounded Knee;
always behind all that is troublesome
lurks the Jew,
always the Jew refuses to behave:
organizing unions, boycotting grapes,
passing out flyers,
holding hands out on the street.
The Jew is the one who asks the wrong questions.

The Jew is the one who asks any questions.
The Jew is the one who knows the difference between
smart bombs and video clips.
Yes, the Jew is deeply knowledgeable about lies,
feels in those Jewish bones
when words are used for something entirely different.

But if the Jew does not sign the loyalty oath the Jew does not teach.
But if the Jew does not pay war taxes the Jew does not sleep.
But if the Jew does not change their name the Jew
does not get into the country club.

But if the Jew does not remember that when they
needed a visa to leave Germany most countries,
including this one,
would not provide;
but if the Jew does not remember hiding in chicken coops and
    bathrooms,
the voices of Cossacks shouting *Where are the Jews?*
Where are the Jews?
the hand rattling the doorknob
the hand shaking the latch
the swirl of feathers and darkness
and the body sliding slowly, gently,
into its own bones;
then the Jew only nods their head
wraps a yellow ribbon around each temple
each home,
each day they watch it rise into the breeze
tossing its yellow reflection
over lawns over sidewalks over windows,
and in the doing
the Jew forgets one other piece of the story,
the one about the great uncle studying the Talmud
who heard those shouts coming closer and closer
and folded himself neatly into the pages,
one by one:
the one that says that the Jew made it out alive.

Full Moon, July 1983

Yes it pulls the tides and launches ships
and strings the light of the sun
to the back of the earth.
But tonight the moon hovers over roofs and sidewalks,
pinpoints me in light
between buildings,
walking the curve of the asphalt skin.

And for one moment I pretend
that I walk the skin of sand and water.
And for one moment I pretend
that my feet do not break that old old skin.
And for one moment I pretend
that I walk and walk
through an endless white and gold night
and do not think about this new death that is now walking with me.

I do not think about the phone call.
I do not think about the *oh by the way*.
I do not think about those glasses of wine
or those ridiculous words
or that walk to a window
to look at a strangely lit sky.

Oh moon moon,
moon full of light and death,
moon shining over me
as if being pretty is always enough:
lower yourself down onto me,
climb onto my shining back,
now that I am no longer just reading in newspapers
carry me someplace far from all the awfulness
we both know is yet to come.

Part of My History

Charlie calls me from San Francisco,
and because I am at work I delete a page from the computer
instead of the paragraph I intended;
because I am at work I press the phone
into the right side of my skull
and I do not raise my voice
and I do not notice that my fingers are on the wrong keys;
because I am at work I say only one syllable words
like *No* and *Oh no* and *Oh hell no*
because No, Lenny, I did not know
and this is no way to find out.
And Lenny, it's been 6 years since I've seen you
and if it wasn't for this it might be another 6
before I did again
but now 6 years is a luxury that I just don't have.

So I hang up with Charlie and I'm retyping the page
and I'm thinking about you like I haven't in a long long time
and the next day I tell a friend
and he says it must be like this when you get old
and hear about people you once knew
who are dying or already dead
and bits and pieces come flashing back,
because I can't remember the color of your eyes
and I can't remember the sound of your voice
but I do remember the day you appeared
after being in Europe with David:
Lenny and David, that's who I kept hearing about;
David was still in Europe
but here was the mysterious Lenny in his bathrobe
drinking coffee in the apartment I shared with Charlie and
    Kevin;
and when I stumbled still asleep into the kitchen
somehow 10 minutes later I knew that Lenny and David
weren't the happy couple that everyone thought;
somehow 6 months later when David came back
he and Kevin got an apartment
and Charlie and I got an apartment
and you got a dog and an apartment

and then moved with dog into the apartment
with Charlie and me
until the landlord who didn't want dogs
or cats or gerbils or rabbits
and maybe a goldfish
but certainly not a Siberian husky
found out
and it was either you or dog
so both you and dog moved to another apartment
and then I moved to my own apartment
and that's basically it:
the night your dog ate my Vaseline and shat on my books;
the night you did my hair for a hot date;
that cold sleek winter night we drove to Provincetown
and no, this is not a story about everyone dying
it's our story Lenny:
whether it was my age or your age or the age or
that last great big frenzied burst of Patti Smith and
marches and makeup and 3 hours once a month at the food coop
it was our story then and it's our story now,
and neither disease nor death nor any number of years
nor you and I being so separate
can ever take away that one moment
that is as bright and distant
as the light from stars
that reaches us thousands of years
after the stars have already gone dark.

On Testing Negative

My doctor flings open the examining room door
like Liza Minelli strutting her way through *Cabaret*,
kicks up his leg, belts out *Congratulations*,
and expects me to be happy.
He's a good man, my doctor is,
a gay man too,
and we sit in tiny chairs and we talk
about AIDS.

Somewhere between that kick and his walk across the floor
the pulse of the room skips a beat
but only one
then it returns to normal.
Outside I breathe car exhaust
then go home
then go to bed.
The next day I tell people
and everyone says *Congratulations*
and everyone expects me to be happy.

Somewhere between that kick and his walk across the floor
I do have a moment, but it's not happiness,
it's relief:
40, a gay man, cranky and negative--that's relief.
The tiny chair exhales with me
then it inhales decisively
and that's not happiness.
My doctor's shirt is white, so is the floor, so is each wall,
tucked at each corner, starched, waiting.
He's a nice man, a good man, my doctor is, so are my friends, so am I.

40, a gay man, cranky and negative.
Sometimes when I go back to New York,
the city of my returning heart,
I see at my favorite bar
gesturing through smoke and the jukebox
a body rising out of the diaspora of the early '80s.

This is what we say to each other
I thought you had died too;
then we hug slowly,
careful not to disturb other bones,
and always I'm feeling not happiness,
not relief,
but the familiar arms of that old ragged anger.

Diane

Once again it's a late dirty night:
3:00 A.M., New York rises
through the open windows
and I can't sleep.

I think about Eric's letter,
turn over, turn on the radio.

Cars honk down the block.
Romeo Void's singing
about a girl in trouble.
Eric writes that he knows
you would have wanted me to know
but, Diane,
there's been too much of this kind of knowing lately.

Once you told me
you had a job that would teach me a skill
that would last me a lifetime.
So far it has.
So far it's given me lots of things.
Right now it's given me 5 days for this new poem
and dinner with Steven
and sex with Allen
because you were right,
word processing *is* the waiting tables of the '80s.
My question is:
how much difference has this life actually made?
It's still 1984.
The country's still in love with itself.
I know that's supposed to be a good thing
but some days I just don't want to leave my apartment;
some days it just feels safer or I'm melodramatic or both
but then I do
because I do
and when I open my mailbox
there's the envelope
with Eric's name at the return address
and already I know what it says inside.

On line at the bank the numbers flash
where to go when the appropriate time comes.
An old woman stands in front of me,
her eyes squinting at the lighting and unlighting,
her bankbook clutched in her hand
as if that alone will provide reassurance
when she reaches her destination.
Her knuckles have brown splotches all over them
and I'm thinking about the two of us
walking through Harvard Square
talking about how the world we knew was disintegrating
and then you told me about the melanoma;
or later, when I was in the lap of New York,
pretending the country stopped at 14th Street:
I was crossing lower Broadway
and saw you and Eric walking toward me,
your hair blowing wild
your skin red from the cold,
and I didn't even know you were down for the weekend.

Now I'm seeing how everything lines itself up
but it's only afterward that we become aware of it.
Leaving the bank I kept hearing your voice on the phone
offering this new job
or me asking when I could start
or that last, cold moment on Broadway, calling out your name.

People were walking around us
cars were stopping and starting
our breath hung in our faces
your hair blew into my eyes.

You said you were going to cut it
so you could go bald stylishly
then asked if I had heard from Rick.
I hadn't,
said he'd just disappeared,
and Mario, I said, I hadn't seen him either.
Now I know what we didn't know then
but then you said something about Rick and his wig
and we laughed about that and the whole thing,

the wind blowing down Broadway
just like our futures:
cold and invisible
and swirling around us
as we hugged and smiled
the way we smile in recognition of something completely
   unexpected,
not at all what we thought we'd get from life
when we woke up that morning.

Avenue E

is not an avenue on the island of Manhattan,
and the insistent lick of the East River or the East River Drive
can't ever make it one.
On the far side of that river a real Avenue E exists--
but that meant Brooklyn,
and we never went there, Steven,
because for us Manhattan was the point of all those years;
not the Empire State Building or Chrysler Building
but out on the edges,
where those crumbling restaurants served borscht bialies and a
  window seat
and were always the first stop of the night:
the beets dunked in red liquid,
the waiter smiling,
the background hiss of cigarettes and voices
and everyone dressed with a particular purpose;
walking down the street with a warm stomach
past bookstores and clothing shops,
cars trucks and taxis honking and bouncing
and the smiles and the looks and the stopping to chat;
walking through those moldy doors
into the kiss of a drag queen and
Lou Reed singing about fishnets, lipstick:
long earrings on the boys,
black pumps on the girls,
wandering from one tiny room back into the other
nodding at familiar faces, drinking scotch and eyeing the
  bartender
when Daniel, who I had cruised for six months,
slipped up behind me and cooed over the music
that he was putting you in my safe-keeping
then slipped away.

Four months later we were at your apartment,
drunk, killing roaches with our cigarettes;
you went out for a carton
and Daniel sat on my lap and began kissing me:
I don't know if it was the alcohol
or the fact that we were finally, actually, doing it

but we kept bursting out laughing and then we just couldn't stop:
Daniel leaned his head on my shoulder,
I leaned mine on his,
and we shook and laughed and kissed each other's necks
until we heard footsteps that could only be yours on the landing below;
when you opened the door he was in the kitchen washing dishes
and I was in the living room changing the record:
it was Marianne Faithfull, she was singing "Broken English,"
and we screamed the words out at each other
while Daniel swayed back and forth between us;
then he kissed you full on the lips, you put your arms around
   him and me,
I put mine around the two of you
and I don't remember how long we stayed like that
or who it was that moved first
but I do remember that when I closed the street door
and stood on the sidewalk
the sky was grey and turning over me
and the streets were flicking slowly open:
empty and a little more promising.

One night you and I were at my apartment talking about the
   band we had just seen:
you told me you had had an affair with the drummer
then leaned over the coffee table and said you wondered
if people now thought we were having one
because we always left in each other's company.
This was long after you had shown me the first issue of *Avenue E*,
told me how you and three friends had stayed up for a week
to get it just right.
E was energy; E was ecstasy; E was excitement; E was for everyone.
E was poems and stories and cut-out figures and
individually colored drawings all enclosed in a large plastic bag.
Each E had different sayings from tea bags and fortune cookies;
each E had its own special tarot card, its own unique E surprise.
Now you said you wanted to do another issue and you wanted
   me to do it with you.
Of course I said yes;
E would put me in print; E would make me famous;
E would get me, like you, into all the clubs for free.

This was 1982. I was going to be a writer or a rock star.
You and Daniel had just moved in together.
Lots of people were jealous. The Pyramid was still ours.
I would leave work at midnight and we would meet at the bar:
you would turn away from whoever you were talking to,
put your hand on my leg and we would plot
how E was going to change the world.
E would defeat Reagan.
E would expose the military industrial complex.
E would bring visual art and writing together;
it was the vision of E: true egalitarianism.
Eventually the man you had been talking to
would tap you on the shoulder
and the three of us would raise our vodkas and toast the new E era.
Sometimes I'd go home with him and sometimes I wouldn't.
Everyone knew about *Avenue E* and everyone said they wanted to help.
We got pictures of abortions and babies
and poems about families that went nowhere.
You found a fake proclamation from Mayor Koch saying
that no man could be out on the street after dark
unless accompanied by a woman.
We collected ads from galleries; we went to poetry readings;
your neighbor said he would draw the cover:
that night we were so happy we drank more than usual and
hugged in your hallway for a long long time.

Sometimes I would watch you in your leather jacket,
gesturing and smoking a cigarette. Daniel would be off in a corner
talking to someone. People would stop and say hi and sneak you a feel.
You would introduce me and they would ask if we were cousins
because we both had curly hair and talked with our hands.
We talked to each other every day; we solicited more artwork;
one night we laid everything out and realized we had 42 pages
and money for 30.
We called every temp agency we knew and took every job offered.
Every Sunday I'd figure out how much we had
and how much we still needed.
You'd order take-out Chinese and say
you didn't know how you'd manage without me.
I'd say you'd do just fine, it would just take a bit longer.
Daniel would call or come by and you would coo at each other.

I'd turn on my calculator and pretend not to notice.
People began coming up to me in bars
instead of pretending we hadn't met 4 times already.
Sometimes they'd pull me into the bathroom
when they went to do drugs.
When it was finally finished we had a big party and
everyone danced and drank and wrote on a wall
every word they could think of that began with E:
it was the eighties; Es were everywhere.
We made up E poems, gave away E prizes,
Daniel created E cocktails and we drank them extremely efficiently.
I remember walking around handing out crayons for people to
   write with,
putting my arms around you
then making out with someone who is now dead.
Even now I can see him walking up to me
saying something extravagant
about how I looked holding a cocktail and crayons,
taking the red one I extended
and when I smiled,
touching my wrist with his thumb and laughing
pulling me into a chair:
his green earrings shining; his hands stroking my cheeks;
his lips around mine,
soft and wet.

This is the only way I know, Steven,
that will bring him, you, Daniel, everyone back.

AIDS Death #54,911

The last time I saw you, Steven, you were huddled in bed,
blankets piled over your body,
you were shaking and shivering so much
there was nothing that could stop it:
your hands bunching the pillows,
your legs threshing the sheets,
you screaming over and over *Lord I want to die*
please just let me die.

And I sat cupping your head as if that could do anything
as if there was anything I could do
feed you tea hold your hands give you more blankets
crawl into bed and lie on top of you:
my stomach on your back
my arms around your stomach
anything to give you warmth, just a little bit of warmth.

It was summer; it was New York; I was back in town
and you were dying. I could sit in waiting rooms
I could help you in and out of cabs and up and down stairs
I could cook for you and wash your dishes and
get you shrimp lo mein I could wrap your neck
with towels soaked in warm water
talk with you about our favorite poets and
that little magazine we used to edit and
how you wanted to be back in Indiana and
everything was over, everything we knew was over.

It was summer, it was New York, it had been a year
since I had left; and you had buried your lover
and you had lesions all over your body
and when I sat in bed with you,
pulled up your shirt to give you a massage
and felt your spine between my fingers
you started crying about the last time anyone had touched you
and how your parents were always yelling,
coming to visit and yelling, blaming you for everything,
and all your friends had deserted you except Michael and Anne;
and Anne lived in Boston and Michael never touched you.

Now Michael calls me and I still do not know why I am healthy
and you are dead. Then Michael tells me how you died:
in a hospital, alone, 32. Yes I can picture that.
I can picture that or the night we sat on your fire escape:
it was summer, a different summer; we were smoking a joint and
you were telling me about a man you had just met
whom you really liked, you really liked him a lot.
Was it safe to kiss, that's what you wanted to know. Steven,
isn't that just the most awful question: is it safe to kiss?